Celebrate the

Founding of America

with Elaine Landau

Enslow Elementary

an imprint of

Enslow Publishers, Inc.

E

40 Industrial Road
Box 398
Berkeley Heights, NJ 07922
USA

http://www.enslow.com

Enslow Elementary, an imprint of Enslow Publishers, Inc.

Enslow Elementary® is a registered trademark of Enslow Publishers, Inc.

Library of Congress Cataloging-in-Publication Data

Landau, Elaine.
Celebrate the founding of America with Elaine Landau / Elaine Landau.
    p. cm. — (Explore Colonial America with Elaine Landau)
Includes bibliographical references and index.
ISBN 0-7660-2557-8
1. United States—History—Revolution, 1775–1783—Juvenile literature. 2. United States—History—Confederation, 1783–1789—Juvenile literature. I. Title. II. Series.
E208.L26 2006
973.3—dc22
                                                          2005018316

Printed in the United States of America

10 9 8 7 6 5 4 3 2 1

To Our Readers: We have done our best to make sure all Internet Addresses in this book were active and appropriate when we went to press. However, the author and the publisher have no control over and assume no liability for the material available on those Internet sites or on other Web sites they may link to. Any comments or suggestions can be sent by e-mail to comments@enslow.com or to the address on the back cover.

Illustration Credits: © The British Museum/HIP/The Image Works, p. 38 (top); Clipart.com, p. 13 (top); © Corel Corporation, pp. 2, 12, 13 (bottom), 36, 37, 38 (bottom), 46; David Pavelonis, Elaine and Max illustrations on pp. 1, 3, 4, 5, 6, 7, 8, 10, 14, 16, 21, 23, 25, 29, 31, 35, 37, 39, 40; Elaine Landau, p. 40; Enslow Publishers, Inc., pp. 4–5 (map), 8, 10; Hemera Technologies, Inc./Enslow Publishers, Inc./Library of Congress, backgrounds on pp. 3–7, 40–48; Independence National Historical Park, p. 6; © Joe Sohm/The Image Works, p. 16; The Library of Congress, pp. 1, 4 (inset), 5 (inset), 9, 15 (bottom), 20, 23, 28, 30 (left), 34, 39 (bottom); National Archives and Records Administration, pp. 7, 11, 14, 18, 21 (bottom), 24, 27 (bottom), 33, 42; Painting by Charles Wilson Peale, courtesy Independence National Historical Park, reproduced from the *Dictionary of American Portraits*, published by Dover Publications, Inc, in 1967, p. 22; Reproduced from *The American Revolution: A Picture Sourcebook*, by John Grafton, published by Dover Publications, Inc. in 1975, pp. 19 (top), 32, 43; Reproduced from the *Dictionary of American Portraits*, published by Dover Publications, Inc., in 1967, p. 27 (top); Smithsonian Institution, pp. 17, 19 (bottom), 25, 26, 29, 35; © SSPL/The Image Works, p. 15 (top); U.S. Mint, p. 30 (right).

Front Cover Illustrations: © Corel Corporation (signing of Declaration of Independence; David Pavelonis (Elaine & Max); Hemera Technologies, Inc./Enslow Publishers, Inc./Library of Congress (collage at top).

Back Cover Illustrations: David Pavelonis (Elaine & Max); Hemera Technologies, Inc./Enslow Publishers, Inc./Library of Congress (collage at top); Independence National Historical Park (Independence Hall).

Contents

THE THIRTEEN COLONIES
1775–1776

KEY

★ = Important Colonial City

✸ = Site of battle between Americans and the British

The Battle of Bunker Hill

NORTH AMERICA

Atlantic Ocean

GREAT BRITAIN

EUROPE

The Thirteen American Colonies

AFRICA

Missouri R.

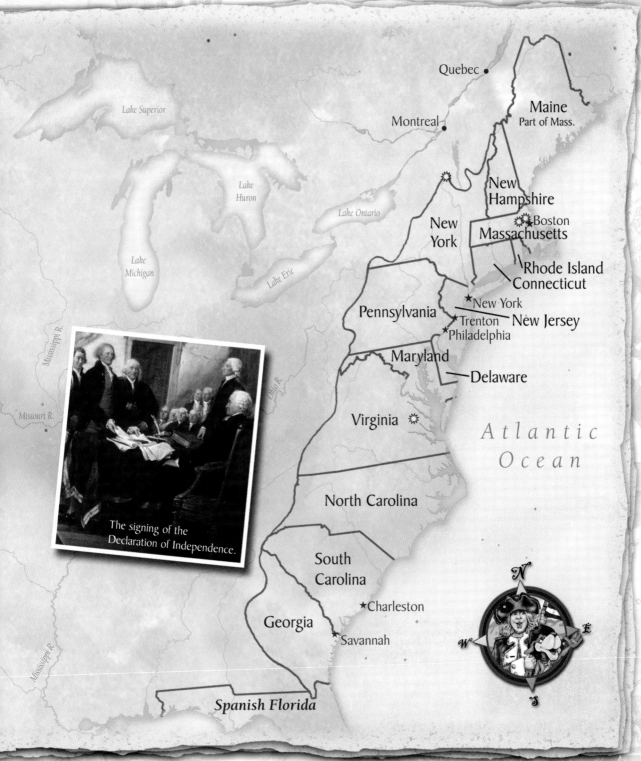

Quebec

Lake Superior

Montreal

Maine
Part of Mass.

Lake Huron

Lake Ontario

New Hampshire

Lake Michigan

Lake Erie

New York

Boston
Massachusetts

Rhode Island
Connecticut

Pennsylvania

★ New York

★ Trenton
New Jersey

★ Philadelphia

Maryland

Delaware

Missouri R.

Ohio R.

Virginia

*Atlantic
Ocean*

The signing of the
Declaration of Independence.

North Carolina

South
Carolina

★ Charleston

Georgia

★ Savannah

Mississippi R.

Spanish Florida

N
W   E
S

Dear Fellow Explorer,

What if you had a time machine? Imagine turning a dial to travel back in time. Where would you go?

Picture being in Philadelphia in the summer of 1776. That was where the Declaration of Independence was written. The American colonists were ready to form their own nation. But King George III of Great Britain was not about to let them go. They would have to fight for their freedom.

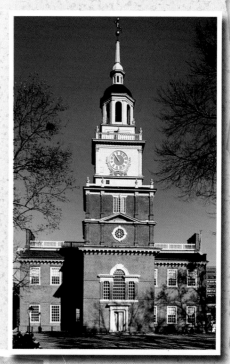

Philadelphia was one of the largest cities in the American colonies.

The Declaration of Independence was signed in Independence Hall in Philadelphia, Pennsylvania.

The Declaration of Independence stated that the colonists were entitled to certain rights. They declared their independence from Great Britain so that they could have these rights.

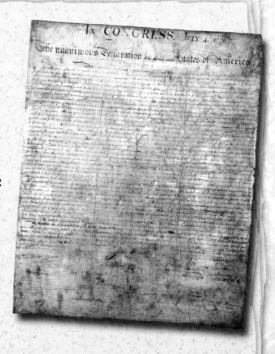

It took courage to sign the Declaration of Independence. Britain was a powerful nation. Anyone who signed might be arrested. Or even hanged. Would you be brave enough to sign it?

My dog Max claims that he would be. He said he would be proud to put his paw print on the paper. Now he wants to go back in time to see what the country was like at its start.

Why not join us on this trip? Use this book as your time machine. To begin your journey, just turn the page.

THEY WERE ALL WELL-OFF AND IMPORTANT MEN. SOME WERE SOUTHERN PLANTERS, MERCHANTS, OR LAWYERS.

COLONIAL LEADERS CAME TO PHILADELPHIA TO MAKE IMPORTANT DECISIONS. I WONDER WHAT THEY WERE LIKE.

1 Tough Times in the Colonies

Trouble was brewing in the American colonies that belonged to Great Britain. Everywhere people were getting ready for war.

BOY, THIS IS HARD WORK.

IT SURE IS, BUT THE COLONISTS WANTED TO BE ABLE TO DEFEND THEMSELVES FROM THE BRITISH.

Throughout the colonies, military groups called militias had formed. They drilled in open spaces daily.

These American colonists were facing a new enemy—Great Britain.

For years, the British government had mainly left the colonies alone. But in 1765, King George III and Parliament began to heavily tax all of the colonies. The Stamp Act of 1765 made colonists buy government stamps to be placed on newspapers, playing cards, and many documents.

Then, in 1773, the colonists became really upset about a new tax on tea. On December 16, they let Britain know

King George III

how they felt. That night, a group of Boston colonists tossed 342 chests of British tea into Boston Harbor. The event soon came to be called the Boston Tea Party. People in other American colonies began to fight back against the British as well.

Great Britain was not about to allow this. British troops were sent to Massachusetts and other colonies. They were there to put down any sign of trouble.

First, public meetings were outlawed. Then, the colonists were no longer permitted to elect their

The Boston Tea Party sent a clear message to Britain that the colonists did not like the way they were being treated.

own officials. The British also ordered Boston's harbor closed. No ships could come in or out. The harbor was to stay closed until the British were paid for the tea lost in the Boston Tea Party.

Angry feelings between Britain and the colonies worsened. At times, fighting broke out between the British soldiers and the colonists' militias. On April 19, 1775, there were armed clashes in Lexington and Concord, Massachusetts.

Something had to be done. So on May 10, 1775, leaders from all thirteen colonies met in Philadelphia.

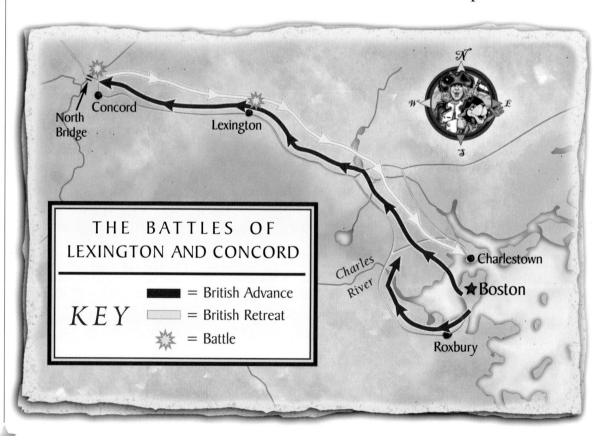

The colonists fought bravely at Concord Bridge. They then attacked the British army as it returned to Boston.

This gathering was called the Second Continental Congress. The First Continental Congress had met in September 1774. That Congress had asked Britain to stop its harsh treatment of the colonies. But Britain ignored its demands.

Now it seemed as if a major war might begin. The leaders at the Second Continental Congress had some important choices to make. Their decisions would change life in the colonies for good.

Here They Come . . . the Men of the Second Continental Congress

In May 1775, the men serving as **delegates** (representatives) to the Second Continental Congress began arriving in Philadelphia. They came from all thirteen colonies. The group would be meeting at the Pennsylvania State House, now known as Independence Hall.

One delegate was a thirty-three-year-old Virginia lawyer and plantation owner named Thomas Jefferson. He had been elected to Virginia's colonial **legislature** (governing body). He was also known to be a very good writer.

Thomas Jefferson was a great writer. His words inspired Americans and challenged the British.

Another Virginia delegate was Patrick Henry. Like Jefferson, he was also a lawyer and a member of the Virginia legislature. He was a man who said what was on his mind. On March 23, 1775, Henry had given a stirring speech before the Virginia legislature, asking colonists to take up arms against Britain. His now famous words were: "give me liberty or give me death."

George Washington was another Virginia delegate. He owned a plantation and had also been active in Virginia politics. Washington did not care for Britain's rules or taxes.

The delegates from the colony of Massachusetts were an interesting group as well. Among them was a wealthy businessman named John Hancock. The British thought Hancock was a dangerous rebel. They were anxious to arrest him.

Samuel Adams and John Adams were delegates from Massachusetts, too. The men were cousins as well as patriots.

Patrick Henry was a powerful speaker.

George Washington had led soldiers before. He brought his knowledge of armies and battles to the Second Continental Congress.

Like Hancock, they had taken part in rebel actions in Boston.

One of the oldest men at the Second Continental Congress was from the Pennsylvania Colony. He was sixty-nine-year-old Benjamin (Ben) Franklin. He was already famous for being an inventor, writer, and statesman. He wanted the colonies to break away from Britain.

HOW COME THERE ARE NO WOMEN DELEGATES?

SADLY, WOMEN HAD FEW RIGHTS IN COLONIAL AMERICA. THEY HAD NO VOICE IN THE GOVERNMENT.

Caesar Rodney was one of three men from the Delaware Colony. Rodney suffered from cancer of the face. He could have been treated in England, part of Britain. But being a rebel, Rodney would hang if he went there.

It is believed that John Hancock took part in the Boston Tea Party.

Along with being in Congress, Ben Franklin was also a great inventor. He was the first person to make bifocals. The lenses of bifocal glasses have two sections. The upper part helps a person see things far away. The lower part helps a person see things up close.

These are just a few of the men at the Second Continental Congress. In the months ahead, they would often disagree. Deciding what was best was not always easy to do.

These men had a big responsibility. If Britain refused to treat the colonists fairly, they might have to break away from the homeland. That would affect the lives and future of all the colonists.

3 A General for the Continental Army

Fighting against the British spread to other colonies. May 10, 1775, was the first day of the Second Continental Congress. On that very morning, New York colonists had staged a surprise attack against the British. In a daring raid, a small group of men captured Fort Ticonderoga from the British enemy. The colonists now had the fort's cannons and ammunition.

Fort Ticonderoga provided the colonists with huge cannons to use against the British.

Colonists had risen up in Virginia, too. There, Lord Dunmore, the British-appointed governor, had seized most of the colonists' ammunition supply. Patrick Henry called together the local militia. The men forced the governor to return what was taken.

Now, the men of the Second Continental Congress felt forced to act. They knew that the colonies needed an independent army.

GEORGE WASHINGTON WAS GREAT AT LEADING THE CONTINENTAL ARMY.

YET WASHINGTON WAS KNOWN AS A MAN WHO LOVED PLANTING AND HATED FIGHTING.

British **grenadiers** threw grenades filled with gunpowder. The grenadier lit a piece of rope, called a **fuse**, attached to the grenade. He then threw the object, which would land and explode near his enemy. Grenadiers wore special bearskin caps.

So on June 14, 1775, the Congress created the Continental Army.

George Washington was picked to lead the troops. Washington was an experienced and respected soldier. He had fought bravely for the British in the French and Indian War. This was a long war fought in America by France and its American Indian allies against Britain.

Washington agreed to be the new army's general. But he refused to accept a salary. Washington believed in what he was doing. That was payment enough for him.

George Washington faced a difficult task ahead. His soldiers were untrained. Some were as young as fifteen. Many had never fought before.

The Continental Army did not have enough weapons or ammunition either. Often there was barely enough food or uniforms. Some men did not even have boots to march in. Yet Washington was determined not to fail.

bayonet

The main weapon of the colonial soldier was a type of gun called a **musket**. At the end of the musket was a sharp blade called a **bayonet**.

The Battle of Bunker Hill

General George Washington quickly left the Second Continental Congress to head for Boston. He was to take over the troops there. Yet even before he arrived, there was more trouble.

By mid-June, the British had sent still more troops to Boston. Warships filled with British soldiers sailed into the city's Harbor. These soldiers were to help the British troops already there.

The colonists were determined to fight back. On the night of June 16, 1775, more than 1,200 militiamen took their places on a hill just north of Boston. While it was still dark, they dug trenches. They made a fort out of thick walls of dirt.

Early the next morning, the British saw what the militia forces had done.

As the Battle of Bunker Hill began, British ships crowded Boston Harbor.

BOSTON

CHARLES TOWN

The militia in Massachusetts were called "Minutemen" because they were said to be able to fight within a minute's notice. Many of them were farmers.

They did not want the enemy to fire down on them with their cannons. So the British decided to take the hill. It seemed easy enough to do. The British had many more men. They were also far better armed.

The militiamen were extremely short on bullets. So every bullet had to count. When aiming at the British, the men were told by one militia leader: "Don't fire until you see the whites of their eyes."

The fighting raged on all day. Twice the British tried to charge up the hill. Both times

Most of the militiamen did not even wear uniforms. However, as the war raged on, Congress formed the Continental Army and started making standard uniforms. Above is an actual uniform of a colonial soldier.

The British soldiers charged up Bunker Hill. As they neared the top, they were fired upon by the colonists.

the militiamen beat them back. The British finally made it on their third try.

By then, the militiamen were out of ammunition. But they were not ready to give up. They fought their enemy in hand-to-hand combat. They hit the British with the butts of their rifles. They threw rocks at them, too.

Nevertheless, in the end, the rebels were forced to **retreat**, or run away, from the battle.

DID YOU KNOW THAT THE BATTLE OF BUNKER HILL TOOK PLACE ON BREED'S HILL?

YES, THE ARMY MISTAKENLY THOUGHT IT WAS ON BUNKER HILL WHICH WAS NEARBY. SO THE BATTLE WAS ACTUALLY NAMED FOR THE WRONG HILL.

The British won a costly victory. Of nearly 2,400 British soldiers, about half were either wounded or killed.

The colonists were proud of themselves. They had taken a toll on the British forces. The Battle of Bunker Hill, as it came to be called, would not be forgotten.

About three weeks later, General George Washington arrived in Boston. He saw that these men had spirit. Now he had to turn these farmers into a real army.

After he was made general by Congress, George Washington soon took over on the battlefield.

5 A Last Chance for Peace

*I*t seemed as if a full-blown war with Britain was just ahead. So on July 6, 1775, the Second Continental Congress issued an important statement known as "A Declaration of the Causes and Necessity of Taking Up Arms." It warned Britain that the colonists would fight to defend their rights and liberty.

However, the delegates often disagreed on exactly what to do. They had many long and heated arguments. Even on the hottest summer days, the windows at the state house in Philadelphia remained shut. The delegates did not want people to hear them shouting.

John Dickinson wanted to avoid war with Britain.

Some delegates, like Samuel Adams, thought the colonies should declare their independence. Battles had already been fought and American lives lost. Yet others, like the lawyer John Dickinson from the Pennsylvania Colony, felt differently.

Dickinson and some others hoped to work things out with Britain. These delegates argued that Britain remained an important trading partner. Many businessmen in the colonies sold goods to Britain. That was how they made their living.

This cartoon shows King George III whipping horses to make them jump off a cliff. The carriage he is in represents Great Britain. This cartoon is meant to show what some thought he was doing to his country by fighting the American colonies.

These delegates also liked the idea of being under Britain's protection. After all, Britain was one of the most powerful nations in the world.

These different delegate views existed among average citizens in the colonies as well. So the Second Continental Congress decided to move ahead slowly. On July 8, 1775, it sent a **petition** (a request signed by many people) to King George III, asking for an end to Britain's unjust treatment of the colonies.

But the King refused to read the petition. He had his own plans for the colonies. These included using force to crush the rebellion.

HEY, WHERE ARE THOSE GUYS GOING?

THE CONGRESS SENT AMBASSADORS TO OTHER COUNTRIES TO ASK FOR HELP IN THE COLONIES' STRUGGLE WITH THE BRITISH.

6 It Is Common Sense

The months passed, and the fighting between the colonists and the British continued. By the spring of 1776, there had been more fighting in Massachusetts as well as Virginia.

More colonists had begun to favor independence. This was largely due to a pamphlet, or booklet, called *Common Sense*. It was written by a former British tax collector named Thomas Paine.

Paine believed that people should govern themselves. In *Common Sense*, Paine urged the colonists to make a final break with Britain. He believed that the colonies could be a shining example of a free nation.

Thomas Paine wrote the pamphlet *Common Sense*, which inspired Washington's army. In another work, *The Crisis*, he wrote, "These are the times that try men's souls." By this he meant that the Revolution was a tough time for America.

Hessian soldiers came from a part of Germany called Hesse-Kassel. This cap from the 1700s was the type worn by the Hessians.

More delegates to the Second Continental Congress were beginning to think the same way. King George III had continued to send troops to the colonies. He hired Hessian (German) soldiers to fight against the colonists. These were fierce fighters.

He also urged American Indians to fight on Britain's side. The Indians were ready to do so. They were angry with the colonists for taking their land. The colonists would have to band together in the coming months. They may even need to find some help of their own.

LOYALISTS OR TORIES WERE COLONISTS WHO DID NOT WANT TO BREAK AWAY FROM BRITAIN. THEY REMAINED LOYAL TO KING GEORGE III.

THESE MEN WERE SEEN AS TRAITORS. THE COLONISTS OFTEN TOOK THEIR PROPERTY AND RAN THEM OUT OF TOWN.

THE SONS OF LIBERTY!

A Revolutionary Year

By May 1776, the colonists had been through a lot. Fighting with Britain, which we call the American Revolution, had continued for more than a year. The Second Continental Congress had been in session for a year as well. Yet the delegates continued to argue about becoming free from Britain.

Then, on June 7, 1776, delegate Richard Henry Lee of Virginia made a bold move. He suggested that they vote to see how many delegates were ready to declare independence.

Delegates from seven of the thirteen colonies were ready to vote. However, the delegates from Delaware, Maryland, New Jersey, New York, Pennsylvania, and South Carolina were not.

The Congress decided to put off an official vote until July 2. That way, the delegates could write to their home colonies. These men wanted to be sure they did what the people wanted.

This is one of the uniforms that George Washington wore.

Roger Sherman helped lead the colonists away from Britain.

In the meantime, Congress prepared itself for what might happen. It put together a committee to draw up a declaration of independence. The writing committee included Ben Franklin from Pennsylvania and John Adams of Massachusetts. Roger Sherman from Connecticut and Robert R. Livingston of New York were to help, too. However, the committee member who would actually do most of the writing was a Southerner. It was none other than Thomas Jefferson.

Jefferson got up every morning before dawn to write. Then, after being in Congress all day, he would write at night, too. He worked at his desk in his small rented room in downtown Philadelphia. Jefferson wanted the declaration to be perfect. It had to stand for what was in the hearts and minds of the people.

John Adams would later become the second president of the United States.

Thomas Jefferson (standing) did not write the Declaration of Independence all by himself. He also had help from John Adams (center) and Benjamin Franklin (left).

Thomas Jefferson wrote the Declaration of Independence on this desk. It is **portable**, meaning he could take it anywhere he wanted.

After about two weeks, he was finally ready to show his work to Ben Franklin and John Adams. They made still more changes to it. However, the delegates had not voted yet. No one knew for sure if they would even need a declaration of independence.

IN THE DECLARATION OF INDEPENDENCE, JEFFERSON EXPLAINS WHY THE COLONISTS WANTED TO BE FREE OF BRITAIN.

YES, HE LISTED THE COLONISTS' COMPLAINTS ABOUT HOW UNFAIRLY THEY HAD BEEN TREATED.

Taking a Vote

T he vote for independence was planned for July 2, 1776. But on July 1, the delegates in Philadelphia took a trial vote to see where everyone stood.

Pennsylvania delegate John Dickinson spoke before the vote was taken. He did not feel the colonies were ready for independence. Next, John Adams spoke. He urged the delegates to break with Britain.

In the end, the vote was split. Delegates from nine colonies chose independence. South Carolina and Pennsylvania cast their ballots against it. The New York delegates did not vote at all. They were still waiting for advice from home.

The Delaware vote was split. One delegate wanted independence while another did not. Caesar Rodney was the third Delaware delegate. But he was not in Philadelphia. There had been trouble in his colony and he had

Caesar Rodney is honored on the back of Delaware's state quarter.

gone back to help. Yet, Rodney favored independence. He could break the tie vote.

A messenger was sent to Delaware to fetch Caesar Rodney. Rodney hopped on his horse and headed for Philadelphia. That night he rode eighty miles through a rainstorm. He wanted to be there for the final vote.

WHY DIDN'T THE NEW YORK DELEGATES VOTE ON JULY 2?

THEY WANTED TO CHECK WITH THE FOLKS BACK HOME FIRST. THEY ADDED THEIR VOTE FOR INDEPENDENCE A FEW WEEKS LATER.

The delegates voted again late the next day. Their vote on July 2, 1776, was for freedom. Caesar Rodney broke the Delaware tie. South Carolina and Pennsylvania now voted for independence too. Their delegates had been convinced by others to change their vote.

Following the vote, Congress made some further changes to the Declaration of Independence. Then, on July 4, 1776, the delegates officially adopted, or accepted, the document.

9 A New Nation

Copies of the Declaration of Independence were sent out to all the colonies. When it was read, the people cheered. The thirteen colonies would soon be thirteen states.

But the story does not end here. Declaring their independence was the easy part. The colonists still had to win the war with Britain. If they won, they would need a plan for a new government.

On July 12, 1776, the Second Continental Congress formed a committee to work on a plan. They wrote a document known as the Articles of Confederation. These were the rules that the new government was supposed to follow.

Meanwhile, the American Revolution continued. The colonists fought long and hard. Many lost their lives. Finally the British surrendered to Washington on October 19, 1781, after losing a battle at Yorktown, Virginia.

The colonists finally defeated the main force of the British Army at the Battle of Yorktown.

That was the last major battle of the war. Over the next two years, there would be small clashes in some areas. However, the colonists had clearly won the war. A peace treaty was signed by the British and the Americans on September 3, 1783. In January of the following year, Congress approved it. At last, the United States was truly an independent nation.

Now the new nation needed a government that would last through the years. While the Articles of Confederation seemed like a good idea, it was not. Under it, each state remained fully independent. It was as if they were thirteen different nations.

The articles gave the national government too little power. It could not call up troops or get money from the states without the states' permission. The new government could not even print paper money.

The Articles of Confederation did not give enough power to the national government.

Clearly, a stronger national government was needed. Delegates met in Philadelphia in May 1787 to improve the Articles of Confederation. However, they decided to create a new plan for a government instead. This meeting came to be known as the Constitutional Convention. The plan designed there became the basis for the United States' Constitution.

The Constitution gave the country a strong national government. Yet the states still had many rights and powers. The Constitution also made sure that the government represented the people. They would choose delegates to represent them.

The delegates at the Constitutional Convention met for the last time on September 17, 1787. That day the Constitution was read and signed. Now it was up to the states to ratify or approve the Constitution. Delegates from each state would either vote for or against it.

Those in favor of the Constitution were called Federalists. They argued that a strong national government was needed. Those against approving the Constitution were known as Anti-Federalists. These included Patrick Henry. He felt that the Constitution gave the government far too much power. Samuel Adams and John Hancock were also Anti-Federalists.

In the end, however, the Federalists won. Rhode Island became the last state to approve

Pictured is an original draft of the Constitution.

the Constitution in 1790. It became the law of the land.

Only a year after it was approved by the states, however, the Constitution was changed. In December 1791, the Bill of Rights was added. The Bill of Rights

states that Americans have certain rights that cannot be taken away from them.

Yet the Bill of Rights did not protect everyone. Slaves in America had no rights. Under the Constitution, representation in government was based on the number of people in a state. A slave only counted as three-fifths of a person.

Over the years, the Constitution would be changed again and again. Slavery was outlawed in 1865. African Americans were later guaranteed the same rights as others in the twentieth century.

Today the Constitution remains an important document for all Americans. It protects our liberty and way of life. The delegates did what they set out to do. The proof is in the freedom we enjoy today.

This collar was put around a slave's neck so that a slave owner could prevent the slave from running away. Slaves were treated cruelly and denied the freedoms described in the Constitution.

10 On Our Way Home We Asked About . . .

Max and I enjoyed seeing the birth of a new nation. The men involved were true patriots. They provided the leadership their country needed at the time.

However, in many cases, these men paid a high price for declaring freedom. Before the end of the war, the British often searched for signers of the Declaration of Independence. They wanted to make examples of them.

Some signers had their homes destroyed. Many lost all their money. Others had to hide themselves and their children to escape capture by the British. A few were sent to prison and some were even killed during the war.

Today, anyone visiting Washington, D.C., can look at the original Declaration of Independence and Constitution.

Both George Washington and Thomas Jefferson are honored on the Mount Rushmore monument.

Yet, in the end, all of these men were heroes. They helped create a country based on freedom. Also, they stood up for what they believed in. The new nation would grow strong because of their courage.

Max and I must be heading home now. But we will not forget our visit to America's past. We are glad you came along with us. Time travel is always more fun with friends. To the time machine!

AMERICA'S FOUNDERS HAVE NOT BEEN FORGOTTEN.

COUNTIES, ROADS, SCHOOLS, AND LIBRARIES HAVE BEEN NAMED AFTER THEM.

What Ever Happened To...

Max and I met some great people while time traveling. Are you curious about what became of some of them? If so, read on!

George Washington

Washington went on to do even more for his country. In 1788, he became the nation's first president. He was reelected to a second term in 1792. Washington died at the age of sixty-seven on December 14, 1799. Few Americans have been more loved or respected.

This bronze medal was made during the American Revolution in honor of George Washington.

Thomas Jefferson

Thomas Jefferson continued to serve the public for much of his life. In 1779, he was elected Governor of Virginia. Later on, he served as Secretary of State. Then, in 1801, he became the third president of the United States. Following his presidency, he founded the University of Virginia.

Thomas Jefferson

Thomas Jefferson died at the age of eighty-three on July 4, 1826, at his Virginia home.

Benjamin Franklin

Franklin remained a devoted public servant and much more. He was also a publisher and inventor. Franklin became famous for his experiments with electricity. He died at the age of eighty-four on April 17, 1790.

BY THE WAY, WHATEVER HAPPENED TO JOHN HANCOCK? HIS EXTRA-LARGE SIGNATURE ON THE DECLARATION OF INDEPENDENCE MADE HIM FAMOUS.

HE CONTINUED IN PUBLIC SERVICE AND BECAME GOVERNOR OF MASSACHUSETTS.

Though historians are unsure it really happened, many people believe that Franklin proved that lightning is a form of electricity by flying a kite during a thunderstorm. This is a very dangerous experiment that no one should try today!

Farewell Fellow Explorer,

Just wanted to take a moment to tell you a little about the real "Max and me." I am a children's book author and Max is a small, fluffy, white dog. I almost named him Marshmallow because of how he looks. However, he seems to think he's human—so only a more dignified name would do. Max also seems to think that he's a large, powerful dog. He fearlessly chases after much larger dogs in the neighborhood. Max was thrilled when the artist for this book drew him as a dog several times his size. He felt that someone in the art world had finally captured his true spirit.

In real life, Max is quite a traveler. I've taken him to nearly every state while doing research for different books. We live in Florida, so when we go north, I have to pack a sweater for him. When we were in Oregon, it rained and I was glad I brought his raincoat. None of this gear is necessary when time traveling. My "take off" spot is the computer station and, as always, Max sits faithfully by my side.

Best Wishes,
Elaine & Max
(a small dog with big dreams)

Some of America's Founders

Name	Job	What He Did for America
John Adams	lawyer	Leader in the American Revolution, signer of the Declaration of Independence, and the second president of the United States.
Samuel Adams	tax-collector	Leader in the American Revolution, signer of the Declaration of Independence, and governor of Massachusetts.
Ben Franklin	inventor/publisher	Devoted public servant, signer of the Declaration of Independence, and an important ambassador for the United States.
John Hancock	businessman	Leader in the American Revolution, signer of the Declaration of Independence, and governor of Massachusetts.
Patrick Henry	lawyer	Outstanding speaker and statesman and an important patriot in the American Revolution.
Thomas Jefferson	lawyer	Wrote and signed the Declaration of Independence, secretary of state, and the third president of the United States.
George Washington	planter	Leader of the Continental Army, signer of the Declaration of Independence, and the first president of United States.

Timeline

1765   The Stamp Act forces colonists to buy government stamps to place on many items.

1773   **December 16**—The Boston Tea Party takes place.

1774   **September**—The First Continental Congress opens.

1775   **March 23**—Patrick Henry gives a stirring speech before the Virginia legislature.

April 19—The battles at Lexington and Concord are fought.

May 10—The Second Continental Congress opens; the colonists capture the British-controlled Fort Ticonderoga.

June 16—The battle on Breed's Hill (later known as the Battle of Bunker Hill) takes place.

July 6—The Second Continental Congress issues the statement known as "A Declaration of the Causes and Necessity of Taking Up Arms."

July 8—The Second Continental Congress sends their demands to King George III.

1776   **June 7**—Richard Henry Lee of Virginia suggests that the delegates of the Second Continental Congress vote to see where they stand on the question of independence.

July 1—The Second Continental Congress takes a trial vote on independence.

July 2—The Second Continental Congress votes for independence.

July 4—The Second Continental Congress officially adopts the Declaration of Independence.

1781   **March 1**—The Articles of Confederation are approved by the states.

October 19—The British surrender to General George Washington at Yorktown, Virginia.

1783   **September 3**—The British and Americans sign a peace treaty.

1787   **May**—The Constitutional Convention meets.

September 17—The U.S. Constitution is signed.

1790   Rhode Island becomes the final state to ratify or approve the Constitution.

1791   **December**—The Bill of Rights is added to the Constitution.

Words to Know

ammunition—Something that can be fired from a weapon, such as bullets.

bayonet—A sharp blade at the end of a musket.

constitution—A set of laws that tells how a government is organized and run.

delegates—People sent to meetings to represent others.

fuse—A piece of rope on a colonial grenade that was lit and burned until it reached gunpowder. Once the fire touched the gunpowder the grenade would explode.

grenadier—British soldiers who wore special bearskin caps. They lit and threw grenades filled with gunpowder, which would explode near their enemies.

legislature—A government body that makes laws.

liberty—Freedom, or the right to do as one pleases.

militia—A group of citizens used in emergencies who are trained to fight.

musket—A gun with a long barrel that was used before the rifle.

outlaw—To forbid something by law.

Parliament—The British section of government that makes laws.

patriot—Someone who loves and defends his or her country.

petition—A document, signed by many people, asking those in power to change something.

plantation—A large farm.

portable—Can be easily moved from place to place.

rebellion—The act of taking up arms to fight against the government.

seize—To take or capture a person or property.

signers—People who sign a document, such as the Declaration of Independence.

statesman—An individual skilled in the ways of government.

tax—Money paid by people to support the government.

treason—Betrayal of one's country.

unjust—Unfair.

Further Reading

Burgan, Michael. *The Declaration of Independence.* Minneapolis, Minn.: Compass Point Books, 2001.

Furgung, Kathy. *The Declaration of Independence and Benjamin Franklin of Pennsylvania.* New York: Powerkids Press, 2002.

Oberle, Lora Polak. *The Declaration of Independence.* Mankato, Minn.: Bridgestone Books, 2002.

Sherrow, Victoria. *Thomas Jefferson.* Minneapolis, Minn.: Lerner Books, 2002.

Swain, Gwenyth. *Declaring Freedom: A Look at the Declaration of Independence, the Bill of Rights, and the Constitution.* Minneapolis, Minn.: Lerner Books, 2004.

This famous painting by John Trumbull shows the signing of the Declaration of Independence.

Web Sites

Biographies of the Founding Fathers

This site will tell you about 103 of America's Founding Fathers.

<http://www.colonialhall.com>
To the left, click on "Biographies."

The Charters of Freedom—Declaration of Independence

Check out this Web site to learn more about the Declaration of Independence. It links to other documents from this period in history as well.

<http://www.archives.gov >
Under "Explore and Interact," click on "National Archives Experience." At top, click on "Charters of Freedom." Then, click on "Declaration of Independence."

The Constitution for Kids

This site describes the history of the Constitution and the Bill of Rights. It also explains how the Constitution works.

<http://www.usconstitution.net>
Under "The United States Constitution" look for the line that begins with "For Kids." On that same line, click on "4th—7th Grade."

Index